BLUE PETER SPECIAL ASSIGNMENT

Rome, Paris and Vienna

D1637695

Blue Peter Special Assignment

ROME:	Film Cameraman	Ian Hilton
	Sound Recordist	Peter Edwards
	Director	Edward Barnes

PARIS:	Film Cameraman	Bob Sleigh
	Sound Recordist	Malcolm Hill
	Director	David Brown

VIENNA:	Film Cameraman	Ken Westbury B.S.C.
	Sound Recordist	Ron Brown
	Director	Edward Barnes

| | Research by | Dorothy Smith |
| | Producer | Edward Barnes |

BLUE PETER
SPECIAL ASSIGNMENT

Rome, Paris and Vienna

EDWARD BARNES AND DOROTHY SMITH

---

*Illustrated with sixteen full colour photographs and with
drawings by Margaret Power*

A Piccolo Original

PAN BOOKS LTD
LONDON

First published 1973 by Pan Books Ltd,
33 Tothill Street, London SW1
by arrangement with the British Broadcasting
Corporation.

ISBN 0 330 23478 1

2nd Printing 1973
3rd Printing 1973

Made and printed in Great Britain by
Cox & Wyman Ltd, London, Reading and Fakenham

HELLO THERE!

Every year I've been on Blue Peter, something unexpected and different has turned up just when I was least expecting it.

For instance, two years ago I suddenly found myself on an aeroplane of the Queen's Flight, heading for East Africa with Princess Anne.

Last year when I was busy working on our Christmas programme, I was asked if I would like to set off as a Roving Reporter on six Blue Peter Special Assignments. The locations were to be six different capital cities of Europe, and the assignments were to find out all about what is going on in the cities today, and to discover some of the real-life tales of the past that made each particular city great.

As my favourite things have always been travel, meeting people and investigating true stories, I leapt at the chance. This books tells the stories of three of the films we made, and some of the peculiar behind-the-scene events that always seem to happen when I'm out with Blue Peter Cameras.

If you're lucky enough to be able to travel, you'll be able to visit Rome, Paris, and Vienna for yourself; if not, I hope you'll enjoy them through my eyes, in these Blue Peter Special Assignments.

Valerie Singleton

ROME

There is a legend which says that Mars who was the god of war once came down to earth because he had fallen in love with a human princess, called Rhea Silva. She gave birth to twin sons called Romulus and Remus, and because her jealous relatives were afraid that the twins would grow up and become kings, they made a plot to drown them in the River Tiber. But their cradle was washed up on the banks of the river, and a she-wolf found the babies. She took them back to her lair, and there she cared for them and suckled them as if they had been her own cubs. The twins survived and grew up to be warlike leaders like Mars their father. They started to build a great city on the banks of the Tiber, but the twins quarrelled, and Remus was killed by his brother Romulus, who became the supreme ruler – and the city on the banks of the Tiber was named after him.

It was called the City of Rome.

Ancient Rome is everywhere

Rome is called the Eternal City – it has stood for nearly three thousand years – and there are still buildings standing, from all those ages ago. Ancient Rome is everywhere – wherever you look, on every street corner, you can see ancient ruins and walls and carved archways. In Britain, if we find a few tiles of a Roman pavement, or some broken scraps of Roman pottery, we preserve them carefully in a museum as precious treasures. In Rome, there are so many Roman remains it is quite embarrassing – when they build a new road, they have to clear the ancient bricks away by the cartload. There is a complete hill made out of broken Roman storage jars! When they built the Rome Central Station, one of the most modern in Europe, pillars from a two thousand year old Roman baths kept getting in the way.

All these old buildings and historic ruins are far too important to pull down, and a network of streets has grown up round them; narrow, twisted, incredibly confusing. And through these streets, somehow, the traffic of modern Rome has to find its way. With blaring hooters and screeching brakes, the Roman driver today realizes just how much the pattern of his city was shaped two thousand years ago. Perhaps that explains why my strongest impressions of Rome were the ruins everywhere, and the screaming non-stop traffic!

On all the public buildings and notices in Rome – even on the dustcarts and the sewers – you see the initials SPQR. These are the initials of the Rome town council, as we have GLC on public notice boards in London. But in Rome there's a difference. SPQR stands for Senatus Populusque Romanus, which is Latin for the Senate and people of Rome. Two thousand years ago it meant not only a city council, but the seat of the government of the whole of the known world.

The Roman legions carried their standards South to Africa, East beyond Mesopotamia, West to Portugal and North to the bleak cold shores of Britain and the borders of Scotland, one of the most unpopular postings in the Roman Army. Yet everything was governed from Rome, the centre of the world. And the centre of Rome itself was the Forum, more powerful in its day than the White House or the Kremlin or the Palace of Westminster.

The Forum still stands there today – a great sprawling heap of pillars and arches in the centre of modern Rome. I walked along the main street treading the very stones cut by the slaves brought back from the campaigns. The Blue Peter camera filming me was high up on the Capitol where Julius Caesar was assassinated by his friends Brutus and Cassius who thought he had too much power.

Walking along, telling this story out loud, I got some peculiar looks from the tourists who couldn't see the Blue Peter camera up on the hill and wondered why I

The Forum

was talking to myself about ancient Rome. But I pressed on to the market place, where once a crowd had gathered to hear Caesar's loyal friend Mark Antony speak at Caesar's funeral. The crowd took the body down to a temple that Caesar himself had had built, and a great fire was made. The body was burnt while the crowd snatched firebrands from the funeral pyre, and rushed away to set fire to the houses of Caesar's assassins, Brutus and Cassius.

Julius Caesar was victorious in death. Caesar – once a family name – was now used to mean Emperor! Every Emperor for the next four hundred years was called Caesar.

The Empire continued to expand, and the riches from the Empire poured back to Rome, to make the Mother City ever more beautiful and sophisticated for the ancient Romans. They had a civilization two thousand years ago that would rival ours today, and they had no labour problems. From every occupied country the Romans brought back slaves. The grandeur of Rome was founded on slave labour. The slaves built the palaces, served at the feasts, and even heated the water that was used in the public baths.

The Romans had a passion for bathing. There were eleven public baths in Rome, and the Baths of Diocletian were the biggest. They covered 130,000 square yards and the many rooms and courtyards could cope with 3,000 bathers at once. The soaring walls are still standing, even part of the vaulted roof remains, and as I walked through the empty halls I imagined them crowded with Roman bathers. The sheer walls, built from millions of tiny Roman bricks, must be nearly a hundred feet high. In Roman times the whole lot would have been faced with gleaming white marble.

The baths were not just a place to come for a swim or a wash. They were the national recreation centres – park, club, library and concert hall all rolled into one. Even the straightforward bathing part was more luxurious than most modern municipal baths. You began in the tepidarium – a room gently heated by pipes, not too cold, and not too hot, tepid in fact. Then you moved on to the Calidarium, a room which was definitely hot. The next room, the Laconicum, was even hotter – and when the bathers couldn't stand it any longer they plunged into the Frigidarium, an open air pool of Crystal Palace proportions, covering 33,000 square yards.

Was it mixed bathing or not? Well, sometimes it was and sometimes it wasn't. The Roman Empire endured for more than four hundred years, and fashions changed, as they do in our time. You can imagine how shocked your great-great-grandmother would have been at the mini-skirt! There were times when men and women bathed nude together but there were also

Baths of Diocletian

times when single sex bathing was strictly enforced.

But it was the activities *after* bathing that made the Roman baths unique. If you were energetic, there were sports, like boxing, with professional boxers you could hire to give you a couple of rounds. Wrestling was popular, too, and young men took part in contests. Both men and women played at ball games – one was rather like baseball, with teams throwing and catching the ball. Sometimes a single player would throw the ball against a wall, and catch it in different ways just as we do now.

Then there were the beauty treatments: you could be manicured, or you could lie on a marble couch while a slave massaged you with sweet scented oils brought from the Eastern Empire. Barbers and hairdressers were in attendance. Most of the men preferred simple styles, with short back and sides, but some had carefully arranged curls, while women wore their hair piled high and elaborately dressed.

You could eat at the baths: refreshments were served as sellers carried round trays with sausages, hot cakes and cups of wine. There is a little bar in the baths today, where the tired tourist can relax, just as there must have been for the bathers of two thousand years ago.

But what I would have liked best, would have been to stroll through the gardens and admire the statues, then maybe to go to a library or listen to a concert; or perhaps, just to sit and idly watch the fountains playing.

The Fountains of Rome

The ancient Romans loved water, and they went to tremendous trouble to bring it to the city. You can still see the ruins of the great Aqueduct which once carried millions of gallons. Water was not only useful but decorative, and the joy of watching the sun sparkling on fountains has lasted the Romans for two thousand years. Every important square, every public place, has its own fountain, some carved by the finest sculptors in the world. Fine poems have been written about them; music has been composed for them. When Rome sizzles in the August heat it's the cooling power of the hundreds of fountains that keeps the city going.

The most famous, and the noisiest and the richest fountain in Rome is called the Trevi fountain. It throws up some seventeen million gallons of water every day, but its fame has come from money – there is a legend that visitors can make sure of coming back to Rome by throwing a coin into its waters. Years ago the

Trevi Fountain

legend ran, 'Only by *drinking* the waters of the fountain can the visitor be sure of his return.' However, as tourists have become more wealthy, and perhaps more wary of drinking foreign water, dimes, schillings, francs and lire are flung into the fountain from earliest dawn until late into the night.

But it is in the afternoon, when the slanting rays of the sun are flooding the little square, that the armies of tourists pour in. They arrive by the coachload, clutching cameras and coins, taking it in turns to click and throw. They come from Japan, America, Australia, from everywhere in the world. I spoke to a man from New Jersey who had met an Italian girl by the Trevi fountain on his first visit to Rome. Now they were married and had come back to Rome for a holiday – so the magic seems to work for some people! The second man I spoke to was from Shepherd's Bush in London, and his job was delivering pianos to the Television Centre – he's often taken them to the Blue Peter studio!

Then I spotted a rather good-looking Italian couple gazing into each other's eyes. She had her back to the fountain with her arms round his neck; he had his arms round her waist. I noticed that his hands held a long piece of cotton, and on the end was a magnet. While the watching policeman gazed wistfully at the romantic lovers, the young man was craftily pulling in the offerings tourists had made to fate and the Trevi.

But not all the money is picked up like this. Every Tuesday morning at about nine o'clock the Assocazione di Fontane di Roma arrives. This is a body of men whose sole job it is to clean out the fountains of Rome. But the money that they find doesn't go into their own pockets – it goes into the coffers of the Commune of Rome. In the week I was there they cleared about half a million lire out of the fountain – that's about £320 in English money.

The spacious Piazza Navona has three fountains – and no traffic. Two years ago the Commune of Rome banned all traffic from the Piazza, and now once again people can enjoy walking in the square. Strolling and sitting in beautiful open spaces has been a Roman delight since Julius Caesar's day. Rome today is a city that's almost killed by traffic, and to walk out of the roaring and hooting into the quietness of the Piazza Navona was like finding an oasis in the middle of the desert.

There were children racing round the perimeter road on bicycles, whilst an old lady dressed in black dozed on a stone bench, a neatly folded cardigan balanced on her head to protect her from the sun. A game of football was being played by four boys, a girl and a Dalmatian dog. Beautiful mechanical birds that

Piazza Navona

flapped their wings and glittered in the sun were being sold, and so were balloons and plastic tubes that whistled when they were whirled round in the air. A pair of lovers sat gazing tenderly at each other and licking ice cream cones. Two hippies with guitars were entertaining the rich diners in a smart restaurant, and competing with them, on the other side of the square, an eccentric old man was playing a mournful clarinet.

There are restaurants and cafés all around the Piazza Navona, and something else that's special to Italy. It's called a *Gelateria*, which means a café which specializes in ice cream, because Italians are considered to be the best ice cream makers in the world. Certainly the one the waiter brought to my table was one of the best I have ever tasted.

The ancient Romans were every bit as keen on ice cream as the Italians are today, but only the very rich, like the Emperor Nero, could afford to eat it two thousand years ago. In those days they didn't have electricity or gas to power their refrigerators – but they did have slaves. Every winter they were sent up into the mountains behind Rome to bring back great cartloads of snow. Then they dug huge pits behind the Emperor's Palace and lined them with straw and leafy branches. They filled the pits with tight packed snow, and covered the whole lot with a thatched roof. The snow was completely protected from the rays of the sun, and it lasted well into the summer. When the Emperor feasted he could have ice cold wine and frozen delicacies like ice cream. Ice cream then was probably made of fruit juice – more like water ices than real ice cream.

When Rome fell to the barbarians the secret of making ice cream was lost, until another Italian – a Venetian called Marco Polo – travelled to China in the thirteenth century and re-discovered the art. He brought the method back to Italy, and the Italians' fame for ice cream has been unrivalled ever since.

Italians are not only the greatest ice cream makers they're also the most enthusiastic ice cream *eaters*, and in the Piazza Navona, I could see men, women and children all enjoying it.

The central fountain in the Piazza Navona is called the Four Rivers Fountain, and it was made by one of the world's greatest sculptors – Gian Lorenzo Bernini. It consists of four groups of figures representing four great rivers – the Danube, the Nile (with head covered, because the source of the Nile was then unknown), the Plate, and the Ganges.

The last figure holds up his hand before his face. The legend is that Bernini made him like this as a silent comment on the architecture of the church at the side of the square. This church was the work of Bernini's great rival, Borromeo, who had also submitted designs for the Four Rivers Fountain. The figure, so the story goes, is holding up his hand in horror to prevent Borromeo's church from falling on top of him. It certainly seems like it when you look at the figure and then at the church. But the Italians have a saying which might apply here: *'Non e vero, ma e ben' trovato'* – 'It may not be true, but it's a good story'!

The Romans love their fountains, and they make good use of them. The waiters from the restaurants in the Piazza Navona draw their water for swabbing out kitchens from Bernini's masterpiece. I saw a noisy group of Italian teenage boys dive fully clothed into it on a hot June afternoon, until there was a warning shout as the Piazza policeman approached, and they fled, leaving a wet trail across the baking square. And the football-playing Dalmatian broke off when he became too hot, leapt languidly into the fountain, made two slow circuits and climbed out refreshed, to rejoin the game without so much as shaking himself.

The Ancient Roman Games

One thousand nine hundred years ago, 1,500 years before Bernini built his fountain, the Piazza Navona was an open air stadium. The road that now bounds the square was a running track. The stadium was called the Circus of Domitian, and there were tiers of seats where the houses are now. Crowds cheered the victories of famous athletes – the gold medallists of the year AD 86!

But the most famous race track in Rome, and perhaps in all history, was at the Circus Maximus. This was where the great chariot races were run, and where the famous Roman charioteers tore round the track. The Circus Maximus is still there, although none of the stands and buildings exist. The track is almost exactly as it was, but pink flowering oleander trees now grow on the banks that once held thousands of cheering Roman citizens. Down the middle of the track there was a strip called the Spina where the presiding judge would stand. Now there's a neat box hedge, and three small cypresses grow where the pillars stood which marked the end of the lap.

I borrowed a little red Fiat 500 and we got permission to drive round the track exactly as the chariot-eers had done 2,000 years ago. The Emperor's box stood by a tight corner at the bottom of the Spina, where he would get the best view of all, and see all the thrills and spills as the chariots hurtled past. The scores, indicating the number of laps run by each chariot, were shown by moving seven bronze dolphins.

The race meeting would go on for fifteen days, with twenty-four races a day, and an incredible amount of heavy betting. The top favourites were four-horse chariots called Quadriga. Only four of these raced against each other, and there were four clubs, called the Blues, the Reds, the Greens and the Whites. The rivalry between them was terrific. They were as highly organized as our Football Clubs, with Team Manager, trainers, transfer fees and temperamental stars. One of them, called Gutta Calpurnianus, started with 102 vic-tories for the Whites, transferred to the Reds where he won 78 times then moved to the Blues and notched up 583 first prizes. He ended a great career with 364 wins for the Greens.

The spirit of Calpurnianus lives on in Rome today. Everyone seems to drive like a member of the Blues or the Whites or the Greens or the Reds. There are no big money prizes for getting there first, but that doesn't seem to worry modern charioteers. They don't seem to understand about pedestrians having the right of way on crossings, either. At least, the motorists don't sur-render their rights until the very last second. I was always thankful and relieved to arrive at my desti-nation.

The Colosseum is the biggest and most complete Roman ruin in existence. In its heyday it was a truly magnificent building, but it was built to house some of the most cruel and barbarous happenings of the last two thousands years: all done in the name of entertainment!

This was the first and largest open air sports stadium in the world. It was built 1,900 years ago, and every stadium since has been modelled on it. When I stood there, looking along the terraces, I could almost believe I was at Wembley, and that I could hear the cheers of a Cup Final crowd.

Every holiday – and there were 170 public holidays in the Roman year – 50,000 spectators would pack the Colosseum. There are eighty entrances, called Vomitoria, and the building could be cleared in minutes. There are no records of any accidents to the crowd during the Colosseum's long history.

Colosseum

Today it's the biggest cats' home in the world. For some reason the city's stray cats have a taste for ancient Roman remains. They lie sunning themselves on marble slabs, play games of tag in and out of Corinthian columns, and hunt for lizards and mice where gladiators once fought to the death.

I noticed that the cats didn't look neglected or half-starved, and I soon discovered the reason why. Every afternoon a tiny Italian lady called Signora Todini arrives promptly at two o'clock. She stands on the bottom rung of the fence overlooking the vast arena, and calls, 'Mishie, mishie, mishie, mishie!' From the depths of the cellars, where ferocious wild beasts were once caged, emerge dozens of purring cats. Signora Todini produces great hunks of meat from a large plastic carrier bag and flings it down into the arena. She doesn't speak any English, so Lodovica, the Blue Peter film unit's interpreter, asked her some questions for me.

– No, she hadn't missed a day for ten years.
– She liked to come promptly at two o'clock so that the cats knew when to expect her.
– Another lady comes every day at nine o'clock, so the cats get two feeds a day.
– If she sees any cats that are ill, she pops them into her basket and takes them along to the vet.
– Yes, she does have cats of her own at home – seven, as a matter of fact.

There are pussy ladies who visit all the Roman ruins – the Forum, the Baths of Diocletian, the Theatre of Marcellus. Every ruin seems to have its dedicated band of old ladies who feed and care for the largest collection of stray cats in the world.

It all looks very lovely today in the beautiful Roman sunshine, but when the ancient Romans sat here it must have been a place of terror. It's hard to realize that where the stray cats now hunt for lizards, fierce wild animals stalked their human prey. This was the place where the Christians were thrown to the lions.

In the Colosseum, gladiators fought to the death, while the Emperor looked on. The gladiators looked up at him from the arena and said, 'Hail, Caesar! We who are about to die salute you.' Then the fighting began. Gladiators fought in pairs, pursuing each other over the golden sand. When one man was down the victor would look up to the crowd to await their verdict. If they all turned their thumbs down it meant they wanted the conqueror to kill his man. The Roman Games ended in death.

Beneath the stage wild animals were kept, and when the signal came they were herded into lifts and hoisted up into the arena. When they emerged into the dazzling sunlight they soon saw what they must do. In the arena, with no chance of escape, would be the victims, men and women. Perhaps they were prisoners of war, perhaps captured members of the forbidden Christian Church. They were all put to death.

This was Rome at its worst. Some of the Emperors encouraged the Games because they gave the citizens of Rome a distraction, and took their minds off more dangerous things – like rioting and plotting to overthrow the Emperor. But eventually people began to be sickened by the Games – socially speaking, the Games were over. The Emperor Honorius actually tried to stop them, but they were too popular with the common people, and he was afraid they would turn against him.

One day a stranger to Rome stood outside the Colosseum. His name was Telemachus, and he was a monk who had given up his life to prayer and good works. He had heard of the savage cruelty of the Roman Games, far away in his own country, and now he was sad to see the excitement and delight of the people. He decided to go in with them, and he quietly watched the races that came first on the programme.

But then the scene changed as the gladiators marched on. In the distance could be heard the growls and roars of the animals waiting their turn. The fighting started. Suddenly Telemachus leapt over the marble barrier into the arena. He turned to the crowd. There was a startled silence.

'People of Rome,' Telemachus shouted. 'You are too good for this! You should not shed blood just for sport. I implore you all – end these cruel games!'

The audience stirred angrily, muttering among themselves. Then one man snatched up a heavy wine cup and hurled it at Telemachus. The rest joined in, throwing knives, stones, whatever came to hand. Soon he was silent, buried under a pile of stones. The games could go on now, but the people did not want to stay and watch any longer. Quietly they drifted away from the Colosseum, many of them deep in thought. The Emperor Honorius seized the moment and wrote out a new proclamation. This was put up all over Rome – there were to be no more cruel games where blood was shed. The people of Rome, suddenly horrified, agreed.

Telemachus was the last victim of the Colosseum,

but he did not die in vain. Today a plain wooden cross stands as a memorial to him, and to those Christians who perished in the Roman games.

The Story of St Peter

Throughout the reign of terror, those Christians who could fled from Rome, just as the Jews fled from Nazi persecution in World War II. Peter, the leader of the Christians, was among those who tried to get away. Tradition says he managed to get outside the city walls, and headed south, along the Appian Way, one of the busiest of the main roads leading out of Rome.

As he was making his escape he saw a man walking towards him, and then as he came closer he saw it was Jesus Christ whom he had seen crucified thirty years before.

'Where are you going, Lord?' Peter asked him, and

Appian Way

Jesus replied, 'To Rome, to be crucified again for you.'

'No, Lord,' said Peter. 'Let me go in your place,' and he turned and made his way back to the city and to the certainty of a violent death. He passed through the Appian Gate to meet his captors. He was taken prisoner and eventually taken to a place of execution beside the Vatican Hill, across the river. It was a place of entertainment, like the Colosseum, called the Circus of Nero, and there Peter was crucified – upside down, because he said he was unworthy to die like his Lord. The circus was outside the city wall, and it is believed that Peter's followers got hold of his body and buried it in a nearby cemetery.

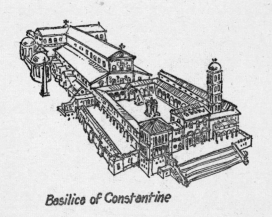

Basilica of Constantine

After three hundred years of persecution, Constantine became Emperor of Rome. He was interested in this new religion and in the end he became a Christian himself. On the site of the old cemetery where he believed Peter was buried he built a great Basilica in honour of the man who by then was known as Saint Peter. Time and the eroding waters of the Tiber began to crumble Constantine's Basilica, until a thousand years after his death a new church was built, literally on top of the old one. There it stands today and pilgrims from every corner of the world go to Rome to visit St Peter's. But although many people believed that St Peter was buried close to his church, no one knew exactly where, and it wasn't until 1940 – thirty years ago, and 1,876 years after the death of the Apostle – that anybody started to look for his grave.

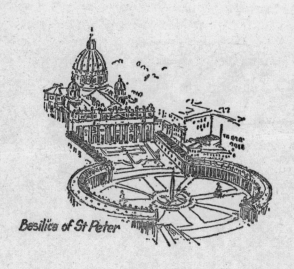

Basilica of St Peter

It all began underneath the High Altar inside St Peter's. Just by the side of the altar there is a narrow flight of steps that leads down into the crypt where many of the famous popes are buried. Pius XI had recently died, and they started to build a tomb for him. Then somebody had a bright idea and said, 'Whilst we're about it, let's enlarge the crypt and build a proper underground church.'

They hadn't been working very long when they discovered the floor of Constantine's original Basilica. This was the first time it had been seen for four hundred years. They carried on digging and beneath the ancient floor they discovered a Roman graveyard. Now they were really on to something – because this must have been the graveyard where St Peter was buried.

Not many people have seen what they discovered but I was very fortunate, for I was taken down under St Peter's by the man who was in charge of the excavations, to re-trace the steps of what became one of the most remarkable archaeological detective stories of all time.

St Peter's - interior

Ingegnere Vacchini* took me down a long flight of steps which led to a small sliding metal door set flush into the wall. He produced a bunch of keys and opened the door. It slid back with a great echoing clang. On the other side of it we stepped back into the first Century AD. We crept along a narrow passage and at last stepped out into what looked like a street.

Ingegnere Vacchini told me that Roman cemeteries were built like streets. This one was about six feet wide with sheer walls on either side. Let in to the walls were niches with statues and urns where the ashes of the Romans were interred. Ingegnere Vacchini said that they sometimes cremated and sometimes buried their dead. There were rooms leading off the street which were mausoleums in which whole families were buried. One of the rooms I was shown held the remains of a family called Valerie!

We were ninety feet below St Peter's Church, and yet when the cemetery was built it was open to the skies. Ingegnere Vacchini took me along to the end of the street and showed me a tablet in the wall. On it was written in latin, 'Bury me in the cemetery on the Vatican Hill next to the Circus of Nero.' This was a tremendous find. It meant that beyond any doubt this was the cemetery next to the circus where St Peter was crucified. And was the man buried here an early Christian who wanted to be buried close to the body of the Apostle? It could be. This was the first positive lead the archaeologists had had.

After months more digging, hampered by underground streams, Ingegnere Vacchini and his team must

* In Italy they call people by the names of their professions, Ingegnere means Engineer.

have been losing hope when they discovered the small rounded end of a pillar. It was the top of an ancient monument. It was the custom of the early Christians to build memorials to their leaders who had been executed, and the archaeologists knew that this was St Peter's memorial. The monument itself had not been fully excavated but you will find on this page the artist's impression of what it might have looked like.

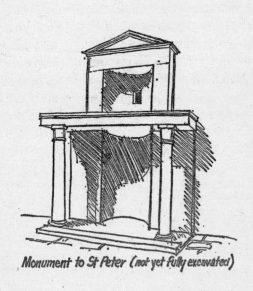

Monument to St Peter (not yet fully excavated)

But was St Peter buried underneath? Nobody knew. They dug deeper and found another clue. They came across a slab covered in writing. The writings were scrawled across the slab by early Christians – they were prayers, and most of them were invocations to St Peter.

It was not very long before a set of human bones was discovered and then the archaeologists checked their position. The bones were directly beneath the high altar in today's Basilica, and *that* altar was built on top of the high altar in the Constantine Basilica. They took out the bones and examined them. They were found to be those of tall elderly man in good health, and many people, like Ingegnere Vacchini, believe them to be the bones of the Big Fisherman, St Peter himself.

Catholics also believe that St Peter was the very first Pope – the rock on which the Church was built; that he was given the keys of the Kingdom of Heaven, and that there has been an unbroken line of Popes from that day to this. Some were saints, some were sinners, some were

Statue of St Peter

great rulers, some were intriguers, some were holy men of God. All of them have ruled over the vast worldwide empire of the Roman Catholic Church.

Blue Peter visits the Pope

Today Paul VI is the occupant of the throne of St Peter.

The Pope is also the ruler of a small independent state called the Vatican. Once you pass through the archway that leads into the Vatican you leave Italy and enter one of the smallest countries in the world. On guard at the gates are the Pope's personal army, the Swiss Guards. A Pope raised an army in Switzerland 450 years ago and there have been Swiss Guards at the Vatican ever since. Their uniform has not changed for centuries.

The Vatican is totally independent. It has its own Civil Service, and its own Cabinet called the Curia. It has its own newspaper, its own radio station, and its own army.

Almost every Sunday the Pope appears at his window to bless the crowds in St Peter's Square. During the summer he gives a public audience every Wednesday, when anyone can go to see him. At these public audiences one or two people are actually presented to the Pope. We were very lucky, because the Pope said that he would receive not only me, but the whole Blue Peter Film Unit as well. I'm not a Catholic, but I thought that it was a great honour for Blue Peter to go and meet one of the greatest religious leaders in the world.

I wasn't quite sure what I ought to wear, so I took the advice of some Catholic friends. They told me that at a public audience you can wear what you like, but that when a woman was actually being presented it was normal to wear a black dress with long sleeves, with something to cover the head. I settled in the end for a plain black shirt-waister, and a net thing called a mantilla to go on my head.

The audiences used to be held in St Peter's itself, but recently a great white hall has been built just inside Vatican city. In a way it's a sort of Parish Church Hall for St Peter's. But instead of a wooden hut for cub scout and brownie meetings, it's a magnificent marble hall built to hold the 7,000 people who come here every week from all over the world to visit the Pope.

As we drove up to the gate of Vatican City a tall handsome Swiss Guard carrying a halberd signalled the car to stop and asked me where I was going.

St Peter's – exterior

'I'm Valerie Singleton from Blue Peter – I'm going to see the Pope. I mean I'm going to the Papal audience.' I felt a bit silly but I couldn't think of anything else to say. However the Guard smiled politely, checked my name off the list, and waved me forward.

I met the film crew at the front of the Hall. They had gone in a separate car because of all the cameras and equipment. There were dozens of officials checking passes: more Swiss Guards, black suited Vigilantes (the Vatican Police), and some men in tail coats and white bow ties who looked like very splendid waiters. They, I later discovered, were the men who carry the Pope's chair. This is a great honour and the men called Sediatore are very proud of their position.

We went forward and gave our names to one of the Vigilantes. Edward Barnes, the director, was rubbing his beard nervously. Like me he was wondering if there'd been a ghastly mistake and our names weren't down on the list. The Vigilante's dark eyes flashed suspiciously down his papers – then he smiled and said, 'Valerie Singeltone and the Gruppa from BBC Blue Petro. *Va Bene*. Thees way per favore.' And he led us down the broad main aisle of the vast and beautiful hall to our special seats right in front of the main audience.

The place was packed with people from all over the world. Indians in saris, a group of Japanese nuns, a block of crew-cut American Baptists and a dark suited contingent from the Church of England. It wasn't at all like waiting for a religious service to begin. It was more like waiting for a pop star or a king or a great hero. There was a tremendous air of excitement and anticipation. Some groups spontaneously burst into

33

hymns conducted by energetic nuns, others were checking and loading their cameras, most, like me, were just sitting waiting for the moment to arrive.

Then our dark eyed Vigilante motioned the Blue Peter cameraman to get into position. A ripple went through the waiting 7,000, and a tiny white figure carried high on a chair appeared at the far end of the hall. The ripple became a roar of thunderous applause as the whole audience rose clapping and cheering. 'Viva El Papa!' shouted the Spanish Group. And the Pope leaned out of his chair and waved. He was leaning and waving and scattering his blessings with such enthusiasm that at times he looked as though he would topple out of his chair into the arms of the applauding crowd.

At last the Sediatore set the Pope down, and he walked up onto the dais where there was a large throne-like chair. He turned at the top of the steps and waved again – and the crowd went mad. Then he sat down and spoke to the audience first in Italian, then in Spanish and French followed by English and German. When he spoke he greeted various groups in their own language like 'The group from the Detroit Mattress Company'. The group cheered and waved, and the Pope waved back.

At the end he rose and gave his blessing. Then he walked down the steps towards the Blue Peter group. When he was standing in front of us I was surprised to see that he was only about my height. I don't know why but one always expects world leaders to be six feet tall. Edward Barnes presented me. The Pope smiled and we shook hands and bowed. Then suddenly one of the Cardinals handed him a piece of paper – both Blue Peter cameras were turning, but what about the sound? We hadn't expected a speech. Quick as a flash Peter Edwards, the sound recordist, produced a microphone from behind his back. None of us realized he'd got it. ('I had a feeling something like that might happen, so had a mike behind my back just in case,' he told us later.) The Pope calmly waited for everything to be in position – as if we'd rehearsed it twenty times and then began:

We are very happy to have this occasion offered by the British Broadcasting Corporation to send our greetings to the children of Great Britain.

Dear Children we wish you to know that you are close to us. We wish you to know of our deep affection for you in the Lord. We pray that God will keep you always in his love and care and prepare you for your life's work. We greet also your families and all your loved ones and give you all our special blessing.

There was a pause and I said, 'Thank you very much, Your Holiness.' The Pope smiled. 'You are welcome. Come again.'

Then he moved off to meet all the people in the front rows. The Indians, the Japanese nuns, the crew-cut American Baptists and the sober-suited Anglicans. He kept reaching out to touch the hands of the people in the second, third and even fourth rows. At times he was almost lifted off his feet. He seemed to want to touch everybody because they wanted to touch him. For a non-Catholic it was a strange, un-English and very moving sight.

Whilst he was greeting and blessing the cripples in

wheelchairs the Sediatore got his chair into position at the end of the main aisle. He returned, a small white beaming figure among the busy retinue of dark suited priests and officials, and sat down in his chair. A word of command from one of the Sediatore and the chair was hoisted and Paul VI Pontifex Maximus was borne away, bending over to wave goodbye to the flashing cheering crowd. The audience was over.

We gathered the equipment together and filed slowly out of the hall and into the blazing sunshine of St Peter's Square. The Pope had been driven back to the Vatican Palace in an open car, and the 7,000 pilgrims were climbing back into their coaches or drifting off in search of lunch.

I felt rather sad as we walked past the Bernini fountains because today was our last day in Rome. In only ten days we had tried to cover two thousand years of Roman life, and, of course, we'd barely scratched the surface. I hadn't learnt to speak much Italian either, but I had learnt one phrase: *'Roma non basta una vita'* – 'For Rome one lifetime is not enough.'

PARIS

They used to sing a song at a night-club in London, which went:

> 'Why go to Paris,
> When here in Piccadilly the Pigalle
> Will bring you all your heart can desire—'

But this is not really true. It is precisely because Paris, so near by air travel today, is so different from anywhere in Britain, that for years people from this country have found it a haven of foreign delights.

The pavement cafés, the marvellous food, the world of Haute Couture and the world of 'Oo-la-la!' – all wait to beckon you in Paris.

But that, of course, is not the whole story.

On Blue Peter Special Assignment, I tried to look deeper, and find out a little bit more about what used to be called the most exciting city in Europe.

The Paris of the two Napoleons

The River Seine runs through Paris, crossed by wide bridges and bordered by tree lined embankments. In the middle of the Seine stands a small island upon which stands the famous cathedral of Notre Dame.

Two thousand years ago, long before the Cathedral was dreamed of, the Roman Army found a small village on that island in the middle of the Seine. They built a camp there and called it Lutetia. But over the years Lutetia grew far bigger than its island, and became known by a new name.

By the eleventh century Paris was the largest town in France. The French kings made it their capital, and people came from all over the country to live there. Like most medieval towns, it was not planned; the streets were narrow and cramped. Then an unusual thing happened. In the nineteenth century France had two rulers – not kings, but emperors – who became very powerful. They could do almost anything they wanted, and they both wanted to make the city of Paris a showpiece for the world.

The first Emperor of the French was Napoleon Bonaparte. He was a great soldier who for a time conquered all Western Europe. To commemorate his

Bridges and quays of Paris

victories he began building a massive triumphal arch which he called the Arc de Triomphe. The Arch was also part of his other great ambition – to make the capital of his French Empire as impressive as Rome had once been under the Roman Emperors.

Napoleon

Napoleon built new bridges across the Seine, decorated with Imperial Eagles. He laid out an enormous square, called the Place de la Bastille, where the old royal prison had once stood. Everywhere he encouraged building in the classical style. He even insisted that one of the old aristocratic palaces – today the home of the French Parliament – should be given a façade of enormous columns. Then, he said, it would match the Madeleine, a new church that was being built in the same style opposite, across the river.

But Napoleon did not live to see his plans completed. The disastrous war against Britain, and his defeat at the Battle of Waterloo, put a stop to everything. Even his magnificent arch was left unfinished. For many years the upper half was only a dummy framework of scaffolding and canvas, and it was not until long after his death that the platform on top was finally opened.

Fortunately his great plan for rebuilding Paris didn't die with him. Thirty years later another powerful man became ruler of France who was determined to complete the work that the Emperor had begun. He was another Napoleon Bonaparte, a nephew of the first, and his full name was Charles Louis Napoleon Bonaparte. Though he was not a great soldier, he was every bit as ambitious as his uncle had been.

In 1848 the French people elected him as President of their new Republic, but within four years he had dissolved the Republic and proclaimed himself Emperor. The next year he was married in Notre Dame Cathedral to a beautiful Spanish noblewoman. She

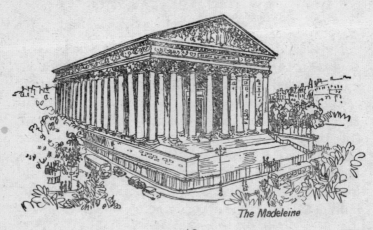

The Madeleine

40

became the Empress Eugenie, and her husband took the title Napoleon the Third, Emperor of the French, declaring that the first Napoleon's son, who died in exile, should have been Napoleon II.

The new Emperor and Empress believed in enjoying themselves, and they began their reign by giving large banquets and impressive balls at the Royal Palace of the Tuileries. They sponsored a great exhibition where everyone could marvel at the wonders of the industrial age, and for a while life in Paris was like one long pageant.

But for Napoleon III this was only a beginning. As he drove round the streets – always at a gallop to give the impression of being busy – he was working out his plans for the capital. These were even grander than those of his uncle, and to carry them out he appointed George Eugene Haussmann, a clever Parisian lawyer, as Prefect of the City.

Haussmann began with practical things. He put up

Notre Dame

hundreds of street lamps, to make the city safer by night. He built clocks into some of them, so passers-by would know the right time. And very French gentlemen's conveniences were another of his ideas. Beneath the streets of Paris Haussmann dug a complete network of drains and sewers, and made them big enough to carry the city's gas mains, the water pipes, and the telegraph wires. You hardly ever see men digging a hole in the road in Paris, because all the repairs can be done underground – by boat!

I went down to see the sewers for myself and I was amazed at the great wide waterways which exactly correspond to the streets above them. There are even the street names on the walls: Champs Elysée, Rue de la Paix, so that the sewer workers know exactly where they are when they are in their dark, wet, echoing world underground. While I was down there I suddenly heard a strange scuttling noise. I leapt a mile, because I was sure it was a rat. But it was a pneumatique. This is a way of sending messages through tubes, by compressed air, just as the big draper's shops in Britain used to send money to the cashier. In Paris the tubes run along the sewers, and provide an extra rapid system of communication for the entire city.

Sailing down the 'Champs Elysée' sewer I was surprised to see a large boat choc-a-bloc with American and Japanese tourists being taken on a guided tour. It is certainly a very interesting place, but a bit on the smelly side for a boat trip, I thought. I noticed that, unlike the boat trips on the river Seine, no food or drink was being served!

Haussmann had another good idea to make Paris a

healthier place to live in. There was an old hunting forest belonging to the Kings of France on the outskirts of the city, called the Bois de Boulogne. Haussmann persuaded Napoleon III to give the Bois de Boulogne to Paris, provided that it could be landscaped, like the great public parks in London, which the Emperor had always admired. Haussmann set to work, excavating lakes and islands in the middle of the forest. He laid out lawns and paths in the gentle English style, and even built a charming lake-side café. The people of Paris were delighted with their new park, and so was Napoleon III. He and the Empress Eugenie often went there in the afternoon.

The route to the park took them down an avenue which Haussmann called the Avenue of the Empress, and it was the first of a whole series of wide, tree-lined roads and squares that he laid out across Paris. To build them, he demolished everything that got in the way, including many beautiful old houses. But he created an amazing feeling of space, and some astonishing views. Radiating from the Arc de Triomphe alone are twelve broad Avenues. The huge roundabout where they meet is known as L'Etoile – the Star.

Haussmann's new roads were able to take an enormous volume of traffic. Even today the traffic in Paris moves faster than in any other large city. It has to be able to stop quicker, too! The rule in France is that you must always give way to traffic coming from the right – but French drivers don't always stick to it! It often looks terribly dangerous, especially where cars from the busy Avenue des Champs Elysée meet the cars going round the Etoile – and it feels even more dangerous when you are in the thick of it!

Looking today at the fine buildings all over the city, Haussmann's rebuilding seems very extravagant. Since then nobody has spent so much public money on Paris. But this was all part of Napoleon III's plan. He believed that if rich people could spend their money instead of saving it, then everyone, even the poorest workman, would benefit. So he went out of his way to set expensive fashions, and the wealthy Parisians followed him. They built new houses along Haussmann's new roads, kept two carriages instead of one so they could attend the Empress's grand society balls, bought new elegant furniture, and wore expensive clothes.

In this way Paris became the centre of the luxury trade, and later on the capital of women's fashion – a position it still holds, even today.

The Arc de Triomphe

I went by taxi across Paris to a boutique run by Parisian dress designer Hubert de Givenchy. It looked a bit like a British dress shop, but there was a big difference. The clothes weren't just sold there, they were made there, too!

I was shown over the building and found it absolutely fascinating. On the third floor Monsieur de Givenchy designs his dresses in a special studio. On the second floor there are workrooms where the dresses are made up And on the first floor is the 'salon' where the finished garments are displayed by a team of models. This is the traditional arrangement of a Paris fashion house, but the strange thing is that it was not invented by a Parisian: it was an Englishman called Charles Frederick Worth, who started life as a draper's assistant at Swan & Edgar's in London's Piccadilly, who created the world of Haute Couture for France

In 1837, twelve year-old Charles Worth travelled from Lincoln to London to take up his job as a draper's apprentice. His father was dead, his mother had had to go out to work as a house-keeper and now young Charles had to fend for himself. In the shop he worked twelve hours a day, selling shawls and dress materials. In those days, few clothes could be bought ready-made. Ladies took the materials home to be made up by their own dressmakers. The fashions of the time seem very ugly to us now; women wore poke bonnets which hid their faces, and shawls that hid their figures. Their stiff dresses were made in harsh contrasting colours that did not go together.

Off duty, young Worth went to London's Art Galleries, at first because they were free but then because he grew fascinated by the pictures and especially by the flowing draperies and rich materials in the paintings of the Old Masters, particularly in those of the French painters. He wished that the women of his own day could wear such beautiful and becoming clothes.

When he was eighteen, his apprenticeship over, Worth went to Paris to find a job. He had only £5 in the world, he couldn't speak a word of French, but he loved Paris from the start. Before long he was working in a fashionable shop in a smart district. His customers were smart and wealthy women but Charles Worth found a young sales-girl called Marie Vernet much more attractive than any of the society beauties. He made friends with her and she helped him learn French. Soon they were married.

Worth began to design clothes for Marie and to have them made for her. She wore them at work, and the customers admired her smart, simple appearance. More and more of them ordered materials to be made up 'In a dress like Madame Worth's' but the old-fashioned shopkeepers were suspicious and disapproving.

So Worth opened his own establishment, in the Rue de la Paix. There were not many shops here but it soon became the heart of the fashion scene. Here he designed clothes – dresses in soft colours, with enormous crinoline skirts, flowing cloaks, new kinds of trimming. Marie wore the clothes to show them to the society ladies who came to buy. This was a new idea – Marie was the first fashion model, and a journalist invented the word 'Mannequin' to describe her.

Wealthy ladies ordered the dresses they liked to be

made for themselves. They were measured and fitted, and the dresses were made in Worth's own workrooms. Worth himself approved of the final fitting. He was now an important figure in the world of Paris dress-making.

A new age of fashion had been born. Worth even dared raise the hem-line fifteen centimetres off the ground. People could now see a lady's ankles, and some thought this was indecent, but the change soon caught on. There was a great demand for his fancy-dress ball-gowns. He sketched hundreds of them, each representing a different character, and he guaranteed never to make the same dress twice. He claimed he could produce one of these at twenty-four hours' notice, though a fully tailored day dress or evening gown took a little longer.

Thus the whole concept of haute couture and fashion had come into being, but Worth still had one great ambition. He aimed to be the unrivalled leader of French fashion, and for this he needed the custom of the country's most fashionable lady – the Empress!

The Empress Eugenie was a beautiful woman. Always exquisitely dressed, she presided over a dazzling court that was regarded throughout Europe as the model of elegance. But one evening at a Ball in the Palace of the Tuileries, Eugenie saw a dress even more striking than her own. She asked the wearer who had designed it, and on hearing the name Charles Worth said she wished to meet this Englishman who designed clothes for the Paris Smart Set.

The very next day Worth appeared in the private study of the Empress Eugenie and showed her his designs. She realized that these dresses, with their flowing lines and beautiful wide skirts, far outshone anything she possessed, and she knew the Emperor would approve of the vast amount of material they would use – this would boost the French textile industry! She ordered ball dresses and day clothes, and she promised to send the ladies of her court for fittings.

The Empress Eugenie

Charles Worth returned to his studio a proud man – he set to work straight away to make the first of many dresses for the Empress of France. The fairytale dresses he designed for her were enchanting – the Empress was thought to be more elegant than ever. Charles

Eating ice cream by the Trevi fountain

At the Colosseum

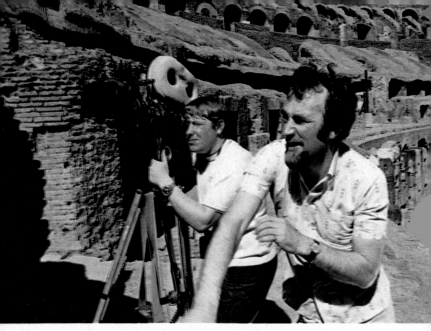

Edward Barnes and Ian Hilton filming at the Colosseum

Looking across the rooftops of Rome

The Pope talking to the Blue Peter team

Bob Sleigh filming me on top of the Arc de Triomphe

Studying the Metro map

Place du Tertre, Montmartre

In Montmartre

Putting the final touches to my port

The Seine with Notre Dame beyond

Driving along the Ringstrasse

By Mozart's monument in the Central Cemetery

With Klaus, one of the Vienna Choir Boys, at the Augarten Palace

A quick hot-dog between locations

Looking at Hapsburg family portraits at the Emperor Franz Josef's desk in the Hofburg Palace; the large portrait above the desk is of the Empress Elisabeth

Frederick Worth, the draper's assistant from Lincoln had become Dress Designer to the Imperial Court.

The methods Worth devised are still used by top couturiers all over the world. In his studio in Paris, Monsieur Hubert de Givenchy promised to show me how he begins to make a model dress. When we arrived, punctually at the appointed time, Arlette the charming and beautiful Press Relations Officer who met us said she was sorry but M de Givenchy would be a little late. In fact, we had quite a long wait, but when we were shown in to him, he gave us his undivided attention. Like all really successful executives, he gives every job his total concentration, even at the risk of being late for his next appointment.

When he got up to greet us I was amazed at how tall he was. He must be about six feet six. I guessed he was around forty; he had a very kind face and a gentle manner. He was wearing a short, white linen jacket and looked more like a successful surgeon than a leading dress designer. I asked him about his life.

Valerie: M Givenchy, what exactly are you doing at the moment?

Givenchy: Right now, you know, I've finished the Winter Collection, the big collection.

Valerie: When are you going to start working on your Spring Collection?

Givenchy: For the Haute Couture Collection, I begin the big Spring Collection around the beginning of November, and I work on this collection November, December and the opening is the end of January.

Valerie: Do you sketch your design on paper?

Givenchy: First I make the sketch of the design, and I

try later to realize the idea with a crinoline or a toile. I don't know how to say that in English.

Valerie: I think we use the word toile, as well.

Givenchy: Toile – well, when it is ready I give it to the workroom, the *atelier*, and later the garment is cut from the toile in the material I choose. I make a selection of material, and maybe I make it in linen or in cotton or in wool.

Valerie: So in a way the toile is rather like a paper pattern?

Givenchy: The toile comes first – before a paper pattern is made.

Valerie: So you make the toile, then you try it out, and then if you like it you make the paper pattern, and then you have the garment made for the collection in the material you have chosen?

Givenchy: Exactly.

Valerie: How many designs do you have in a collection?

Givenchy: Every collection, approximately, I have one hundred, one hundred and fifty sections – in each section you have maybe a two piece or three piece, you have a suit, you have a blouse, you have a coat, or a raincoat.

Valerie: Are you working constantly? Do you go around with a little sketch pad in your pocket, so that when you get an idea you just jot it down wherever you are?

Givenchy: No – I do have with me some little book, you know, to make notes, but when I finish a collection I travel or I try to think of something else.

Valerie: Do you ever run out of ideas, so that you're stuck and you can't think of something to do?

Givenchy: You know, you always have your mind working, but it's sometimes difficult. Sometimes, you know, when I make the collection, I try, try, try to do something, and nothing happens, and suddenly—

Valerie: It comes?

Givenchy: Something comes – a detail, a sleeve, a line, a silhouette, and this is the most interesting part of the work.

Valerie: When you have a collection and you develop a new line, do you like to try and follow that theme through to your next collection, or do you like to have a complete change?

Givenchy: I don't like to change completely, because I think fashion is an evolution, you know, little by little, in details.

Valerie: What do you think is the most important in a garment – would you say line, or simplicity or cut?

Givenchy: I think the most important thing is the simplicity, really.

Valerie: I notice you're surrounded by materials of all the most beautiful colours. Do you design your own materials as well?

Givenchy: Some I design, and some I have manufactured specially for me, in Switzerland, in Italy, in France too, and in England.

Valerie: Do you think fashion goes in cycles? Can you see a time when we perhaps might all be wearing crinolines again, like the Empress Eugenie and her court ladies?

Givenchy: No – and you know, this recent season a lot of designers tried to return to the 1940s. And I think it is too near, you understand. It's too soon. And another thing, I think it isn't a very pretty *époque*, a pretty style.

Valerie: I agree with you! Have you got a favourite period in history?

Givenchy: If I am thinking of the history of costume, I think one of the most precious and refined periods is the *époque* of your Queen Elizabeth, Elizabeth la Grande, because I think the detail of the embroidery, of the colour, of the coiffure, you know, is so beautiful.

Valerie: The last question of all – how did you begin? Now you're a very famous Haute Couture designer – how did you first get interested.

Givenchy: I begin when I am very young – maybe when I am five years old or six years old. I always admire my mother, and help to choose her dress—

I remember one story. I have a very, very good godfather, he is an English gentleman, and he give me one day for Christmas a beautiful Doll's House, and I am fascinated by that house. I have electricity, I have everything in that house, and suddenly I say, 'Maybe it is a good idea to change this doll's house and make a Maison de Couture – a Fashion House.' So this is my first Maison de Couture, when I am a little boy. And of course I have some – what you say – *poupettes*?

Valerie: Dolls.

Givenchy: And I fix some hats, some dresses, it is just nothing, just a piece of chiffon, but this is the first time when I begin to want to be a designer.

After I left M Givenchy's studio, I was shown the place where all his designs are turned into reality – the heart of every fashion house, the workroom.

The first thing that struck me was the silence. There is no whir of electric sewing machines, just the faint hiss of cotton pulled through material, because every stitch here is made by hand. It takes about 150 hours of hard work to produce one evening dress. At a high desk surveying the room sits the overseer. All the work is shown to him for approval. The House of Givenchy is run very strictly according to rules. A bell rings at 1 PM for lunch and again at 2 PM for work to resume.

At 3 PM every afternoon, there is a fashion show in the Givenchy salon. Every fashion house has a daily show, and it is this present-day version of Madame Worth's dress displays that has given Parisian Haute Couture its international pre-eminence. Although the Givenchy salon is packed with rich and famous customers you don't have to pay to go in. All you need to do is to telephone and reserve a seat.

I went along one afternoon, and I took my reserved place on a small elegant gilt chair, marked by a neatly written card saying 'Mlle Singleton'. I glanced at the card on the chair next to me. In the same handwriting was written 'Mme Rothschild'. Also on my chair was a card and a sharp pencil. Each model girl carries a number, so that customers can make a note of a dress they like, and ask to see it again afterwards.

The salon itself is a masterpiece of restrained elegance. The floor, walls and ceiling are plain dazzling white. The only colour comes from the gilt chairs placed on white tiered rostra on either side of the catwalk, and two enormous gilt framed mirrors at either end.

Promptly at 3 PM the show begins, with Suzanne, a

pretty dark girl with enormous brown eyes wearing a green suede hat with green suede trousers and boots and a fur poncho over a beige jersey with green suede sleeves. There was no music and no commentary – just one girl following the next, each carrying a discreet number. Each girl walked from one end of the salon to the other, made what I recognized, from my own model training, as a 'Paris turn', and walked back and out through the door.

Occasionally a customer would mutter to her neighbour, and a diamond ring would flash as someone noted down a number. But there was little noise apart from the rustling of silks and the delicate tread of the elegant girls. They looked very cool, sophisticated and forbidding in the salon, but once through the door into the *cabine* where they dress the cool disappeared in a frantic effort to get the next outfit on. A change isn't just a change of clothes; it's jewellery, make-up and hairstyles as well, not to mention gloves, handbags and headscarves. Each girl wears twenty outfits, ranging from swimsuits to evening dresses – and enormous fur coats.

After the first four ensembles, there is no set order for the models to appear, and the next girl who's dressed goes on. Sometimes there are three girls in various stages of undress, and only one ready to enter. '*Tu vas traîner, n'est-ce pas?*' – 'Take your time, won't you?' is the frantic cry, as the four models, three dressers and a hairdresser fight among the silks and furs, the jewellery and underwear in the *cabine*.

Meanwhile, back in the salon, all is silence and elegance.

Suzanne re-appeared in a gorgeous evening dress

54

and a really stunning black and turquoise silk evening coat which reached to the floor and shimmered like a peacock when she moved. I wrote the number neatly on my card.

The end of the show is traditionally the bridal gown. Today it was a classic long white medieval dress with a long floating veil. As the model drifted between the great gilt mirrors there was a polite ripple of applause, and the show was over.

I went into the *cabine* to meet the four girls as they made their last change of the day – into their own clothes to go home. Although they look cool and forbidding in the salon, and absolutely frantic in the *cabine* while the show is on, they were really nice friendly girls when I chatted to them afterwards. Suzanne told me I could try on the coat I had so much admired. The girls helped me to put it on, and I walked out into the now empty salon, to look at myself in the never ending mirrors. I stood there imagining for a few seconds that I was a Parisian top model, or a millionairess!

Across Paris by Metro

The French take their language very seriously, and they hate to hear it used inaccurately or mispronounced. This makes it very difficult for a foreigner, whose struggles to reproduce school French are met with a 'Hein?' 'Comment?' or a blank stare from the language conscious Parisians. But it does mean that the French *they* speak is accurate and never sloppy, and no-one would dare to alter a line of a classical French play or poem.

This tradition belongs to the left-bank quarter of Paris, home of the Sorbonne University, and of the pavement cafés where so many famous writers have planned their works and where hundreds of years ago Francois Villon, the Vagabond King, wrote his beautiful poems. Today you can buy just about any second-hand book here at a very reasonable price.

The French word for an old book is a *bouqin*, and that is why the men who have their boxes of wares right on the edge of the Seine have always been known as *bouqinistes*. They pay a fee to the city council so they can leave their box fixed up for business. They don't just sell books – they have lots of prints and posters, for Paris has always been renowned for its painters.

But the strange thing is that whilst the writers and philosophers have always lived on the left bank, near the University, the most famous artists lived in Montmartre, a tiny village almost on the edge of Paris, high up on the right bank.

The fastest way of getting across Paris is by Metro – the Paris Metropolitan Railway. Some of it is underground, and some overhead, but however far you travel there's only one fare, about ten pence. For this you could get on the Metro in the morning and ride round all day! I followed the signs up to the platform, and was just in time to catch a train. Most of the Metro was built about seventy years ago – and the first train I boarded looked like some of the original rolling-stock. It was a period when engineers were experimenting with steel, and the overhead spans that carry some sections of the Metro were thought to be quite revolutionary.

So was the Eiffel Tower, which I could see from my train window. It was put up in 1889 as part of an International Exhibition, just to show that a high steel tower could be built. It was never intended to stay there, but when the exhibition ended no one could bear to pull it down. Today it's a symbol of Paris throughout the world, and it proves that when French engineers really get their teeth into something the results can be quite breathtaking.

Once across the Seine the Metro dived underground, and took me to a station directly under the Place de l'Etoile. Here I had to change lines but there was a big illuminated map to guide me. I found that to get to Montmartre I had to go even deeper underground. I went on an escalator that led down to the new express Metro line opened a year or so ago. It's been built underneath all the existing lines, and the whole system has been designed to move a lot of people quickly – so there's no question of walking anywhere and all the corridors are fitted with long moving pavements. When I went it seemed almost empty, and at first I wondered

Eiffel Tower

why, but the express Metro is mainly a commuter line – so it's only at rush hours that it gets busy. I felt that it wouldn't look crowded even then, because everything is so large. The trains themselves travel at up to 70 mph and only stop every two miles or so – but they're so smooth you hardly notice the speed.

I was glad to see that among all the up-to-the-minute equipment they still have room for a curious notice. It is on all the Metro trains and is typically French. Headed 'Places Reserves', it explains that four seats are reserved in order of priority, firstly for soldiers injured during the war, secondly for blind people, and lastly for ladies expecting a baby. If no one in the carriage fits into those categories, then anyone can sit on them!

I'd thought the station at the Etoile was big enough, but at the terminus there's a huge underground concourse, thirty-six metres beneath street level, complete with little shops that look like igloos – so if you don't want to climb up to the surface to do your shopping you don't have to!

I couldn't help thinking that Haussmann and Napoleon III would approve of it all. Once again Paris is planning a transport system much bigger than it would seem to need, but in thirty years or so the express Metro will probably be as busy as their roads are now.

Montmartre

Of course, enormous plans don't suit everyone. That's why towards the end of the nineteenth century many of the painters in Paris found the village of

Montmartre, with its new white church of the Sacre Coeur, so attractive – just *because* Haussmann had never touched it. Its tall houses, narrow streets and steep gradients made rebuilding too expensive even for him, so it has remained an area of old-fashioned charm. Artists like Van Gogh and Renoir, and later Utrillo and Picasso, found Montmartre an ideal place to paint, high up above the bustle of the capital, and they did a lot of their best work here. When these artists and their pictures became famous, so did Montmartre.

The tourists who came from all over the world to see the sights of Paris, all wanted to visit the artists' village. In a very short time the visitors made the place so noisy and crowded that the serious artists had to move out to find peace and quiet! Today the old village square is without doubt the most touristy place in all Paris. There are still artists, but they're more interested in making a living than in painting a masterpiece. There are supposed to be 50,000 working artists in Paris, and

Sacre Coeur

as I sat down at a table in the square, ordered a drink from the waiter, and looked about me, I could well believe it!

Some of them, rather than sell paintings they've already done, wander round the cafés and offer to make a lightning portrait sketch of anyone who's willing to pay. I decided it would be a nice souvenir. The artists usually do a highly romanticized and frankly flattering portrait, but I was lucky – I suppose you'd call it lucky! – to meet an artist who was a caricaturist.

He didn't exactly make a caricature of me, but it was a much livelier picture than I'd expected! He told me there were about a hundred artists working in the square, and that during the tourist season they did very well.

Montmartre today is still very colourful, though I think I might have preferred it in Van Gogh's time, when there were windmills and vineyards. But the artists were followed by tourists, holiday makers, businessmen out for a spree with money to spend. Restaurants, cabarets, night clubs opened for them – the last of the windmills became dance halls, as a new Montmartre, centre of a new entertainment industry came into being. But for a while the artists were still there, and they painted the newcomers to Montmartre, the new artists of show business.

One of the best known of these artists was a sad man, known as Toulouse Lautrec. His full name was Henri Marie Raymond de Toulouse-Lautrec, and he came from an ancient noble family. His father, Count Alphonse, was a wild, eccentric man who lived for hunting, and for his horses. His son loved horses too, to ride and to draw, for from the beginning he was clever at drawing everything he saw. His mother encouraged him in his sketches, for as a boy he was often ill and unable to get about. Secretly she was anxious that he might never be really strong, for Henri did not grow.

In the castle where the family lived, there was a wall where all the children – Henri and his cousins – were measured each summer. *Their* marks grew higher and higher but Henri could hardly tell the difference in his from one year to the next It was a wretched business: the Wailing Wall, he called it.

Then, one day when he was thirteen, Henri, who had been ill, tried to get out of his chair with a stick. He fell, and lay helpless. He had broken his left thigh. Slowly, painfully, he got better. His mother looked after him tenderly. His father was bored and impatient – he had no use for invalids. Henri got over the fall, but

Toulouse Lautrec

still he did not grow. Then, fifteen months after the accident, he went for a walk. He slipped and fell into a ditch. Now his right thigh was broken.

These two dreadful accidents, to someone whose bones were fragile and whose health was bad, were disastrous. The Wailing Wall would show no more growing for Henri. After that he grew no more, he was just under five feet tall, a cripple and an invalid. Worst of all he realized he would be like that for the rest of his life. He knew he would never be strong enough to manage the family's great estates – and though his mother remained as devoted as ever, his father now ignored him. So Henri decided to leave home and take up painting in earnest.

He enrolled as a pupil in an artist's studio in Paris. Every morning he arrived by cab, struggled out painfully, and clambered to the stool before his easel. There, his clumsiness left him – soon he was painting confidently and well. He began to be taken seriously as an artist. He rented a studio for himself in Montmartre, and met the great artists of his day – Degas, Renoir, Van Gogh – and his own work reached great heights, with their encouragement. He hated being alone, and was always afraid strangers would laugh at his odd appearance. He loved being the centre of a crowd of rowdy friends.

He turned away completely from the high society he had been born into, and took as his friends the growing number of entertainers in the bistros and dance halls of Montmartre. The lurid night life gave him not only some kind of pleasure, but also models and subjects for his painting. He began to make portraits of the singers, dancers and comedians who had become his friends. Soon they asked him to design posters for their shows. His strong lines and bold flat colours printed very well, and soon the posters were on hoardings all over Paris.

One of the best known was of the comedian Aristide Bruant, who introduced the cabaret at Le Mirleton. In his act he sang mocking songs about the politicians of his day. Then he would stop and shout insults at the audience – they loved it! Lautrec also drew May Belfort who dressed up like a little girl, and clutched a kitten. She sang mock-innocent songs like 'Daddy wouldn't buy me a bow-wow!'

The great star attraction for the visitor to Montmartre was the delirious dance they called the can-can. At the Moulin Rouge the spectacle was terrific, with the line of plunging can-can dancers and its flaming red-haired star, the incomparable La Goulue. 'Higher, La Goulue, higher!' the crowd shouted, as she kicked her black-stockinged legs and tossed her swirling white petticoats. One night the Prince of Wales – later to be Britain's King Edward VII – was there watching. 'Hello, Wales,' she called, 'Are you paying for the champagne?' For a few short years La Goulue was the toast of Paris, and thanks to Toulouse-Lautrec's posters she became known all over the world. For he made his posters into works of art which are still reprinted today.

Despite his success, Henri remained an unhappy man. He knew he would never be strong, and desperately aware that his life could never change, he wore himself out between work and the search for pleasure. Drink and disaster were waiting for him. He returned home in the hope that his mother could nurse him back to health. It was too late. He died soon after his thirty-seventh birthday.

The noisy colourful Montmartre he loved and helped to create, lives on just the same. Art lovers still buy his posters, and at the Moulin Rouge, over seventy years after his death, they still dance the can-can. Every evening hundreds of tourists go to the village square of Montmartre, just to dine in the atmosphere that Toulouse-Lautrec captured in his paintings.

The Place du Tertre, main square of Montmartre, is very blatantly touristy and trippery, but I think it's got something which you can find nowhere else in Paris. There is here, in spite of the coach-loads of American, Japanese, German and British visitors, a feeling of unselfconscious gaiety, and an atmosphere that belongs only to Montmartre.

The old men playing chess in the cafés were not there to please the tourists, and neither were the old women, dressed in black from head to foot, carrying home their metre of bread, every morning. Who cares if I did look like a tourist, sipping my wine and having my portrait drawn? I was enjoying myself. And so were the other tourists, and the French families eating and drinking at the tables under the trees.

Eating out in Paris is always a grand occasion, because the French really do worship food. They have a proverb that one should live to eat, not merely eat to live. So wherever you go in Paris there is a bewildering choice of restaurants and cafés, all serving exquisite food – at terrifying prices!

But the restaurants are not just patronized by rich people, or by couples dining out together. Food is everyone's treat. Whole families, from babies to grand-parents, celebrate birthdays or anniversaries by going to a restaurant for a delicious meal. As soon as they can read, French children can find their way about the complicated menus – and they soon know how they like their meat cooked, and what is their favourite sauce.

The wealthy business man takes two hours over his lunch – but so too does the small shopkeeper. And every mid-day the taxi drivers go to their restaurant, the Rendez-Vous Des Chauffeurs, very near to the Etoile and the Champs Elysées, to make their choice from a menu that includes Pâté Maison, and snails, and Tripe à la mode de Caen.

They choose carefully, and want the best. If the food is not to their liking, they send it back at once. No wonder the restaurants in Paris are the best in the world.

The Fourteenth of July

Perhaps the most romantic way to have dinner in Paris is by boat. Every evening at nine o'clock a long sleek *Bateau Mouche* sets off for a two-hour cruise up and down the Seine, and during the trip a full-scale candle-lit dinner is served. It looks very smart, but it was far too expensive for me. So I went on a little half hour cruise. We didn't get dinner, but we had just as good a view of the river.

The light was beginning to fade, but fortunately many public buildings in Paris are floodlit. During the summer the lights are turned on most evenings, but even during the winter anyone can have a monument or building lit up specially, if he gives forty-eight hours' notice and pays the electricity bill. You can have the whole Place de la Concorde floodlit for just £5 an hour.

But on my last night in Paris everything was lit up! Not just because it was the tourist season, but because it was the most important day in the French year – July 14th. That was the day when the people of Paris stormed the old royal prison of the Bastille during the great French Revolution of 1789. And it's celebrated every year rather like a Bank Holiday and Bonfire Night rolled into one.

I drove with the Blue Peter film crew along packed streets towards the Eiffel Tower. Cars were jammed solid four abreast along the entire length of the Champs Elysées, but nobody seemed to care – it was Bastille night! In the end we abandoned our car and walked across the bridge to the foot of the Eiffel Tower where thousands of people stood to watch the Paris sky ablaze with fireworks.

Bateau Mouche

The people of Paris have never missed a chance to enjoy themselves. When they'd finished demolishing the Bastille, they organized a dance on the ruins to mark the occasion, and they still dance in the streets every July 14th. For one glorious night Paris drifts back into its own colourful and impressive past. For throughout its history, from the island settlements of the Romans, through the great plans of the two Napoleons, to the wide modern city of today, Paris has always known how to do things in style.

Place de la Concorde

VIENNA

Wien, Wien, nur du allein
Sellst stets die Stadt meiner Traume sein

If you have difficulty in understanding this, think of me trying to sing it in a wine garden in Vienna with the Blue Peter cameras turning watched by a hundred highly amused Viennese.

The words, roughly translated, mean 'Vienna, City of my Dreams', and I was singing them in Grinzing, a little village surrounded by wine gardens on the outskirts of Vienna. There are dozens of gardens in the village, where the Viennese go to drink the *Heuriger,* which is German for 'new wine'. It all looks tremendously gay. The trees are decorated with fairy lights, pretty girls in Austrian national dress are serving the Heuriger, and musicians wander from table to table playing Viennese songs.

Grinzing is a great place for tourists. The night I was there I saw a large party of Japanese, very polite though slightly drunk, all wearing Tyrolean hats with feathers at the back! But it's not just the tourists who patronize the gardens of Grinzing – the Viennese themselves are there as well, and Vienna is one of the few places left in Europe where a man will pay a band to accompany him whilst he sings a love song to his girl friend in a public café!

But who are the Viennese?

Some time ago a Viennese newspaper offered a prize of 10,000 Austrian schillings for anyone who could prove that he was truly Viennese by providing the names of four grandparents all born in Vienna – the reward is still unclaimed for the Viennese are not just people who live in the capital city of a vast and powerful Empire. At its height the Empire consisted of lands that are now part of Czechoslovakia, Hungary, Yugoslavia, Poland and Northern Italy; the people from these lands were attracted to the Imperial capital, Vienna. They settled down in the city and when at last the Empire collapsed in 1918 they never returned to their original countries. Vienna was now their home and they, and their children, have stayed there ever since.

Vienna Woods

Schönbrunn, the Palace of the Hapsburgs

For six-and-a-half centuries, this Empire was ruled from the Imperial City of Vienna by one great family, the Hapsburgs. They ruled and fought, made peace treaties and marriage alliances, and their Empire grew and grew. Their symbol was the great two-headed eagle, master of all it surveyed, gazing from on high on all the lands the Hapsburgs owned, sprawled across Central Europe, a bulwark against the Russians and the Turks. For all this time the countries of the Empire, in spite of their different languages and religions, regarded themselves not as separate peoples but as citizens of the Empire, united in loyalty to their rulers, the Hapsburgs.

The Hapsburgs were a family set apart, believing that they were born to rule and that they had been given their Empire by God. Each member of the family had two duties in life: to put the family first, before self, or love, or friendship, and to preserve the

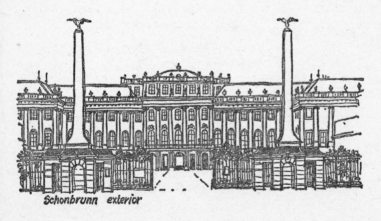

Schonbrunn exterior

inheritance intact for generations of Hapsburgs as yet unborn.

Today the Hapsburgs are gone. The lands are divided and the Empire is no more. But in Vienna, where footsteps echo through the empty palaces, and ghosts walk in the Imperial Parks, I felt all the time that life is still lived in the shadow of that once all-powerful family.

The Empress Maria Theresa

Schönbrunn, the great summer palace of the Hapsburgs is set in vast and resplendent gardens on the outskirts of Vienna. It was begun in 1696 to provide a worthy setting for the court, away from the old dark Hofburg Palace in the heart of the city. It became one of the grandest palaces in Europe. Maria Theresa, who became Empress when she was twenty-three, loved Schönbrunn and called in artists from all over Europe to complete it. She designed its rooms, ordered their decoration and chose the furniture. Above all, she supervised the gardens, with the formally patterned flower-beds, the avenues and leafy walks, the beautiful fountains and statues, all crowned by the little hill and dominated by the Gloriette. This is a gleaming white structure of colonnades and steps, surmounted by the Hapsburg eagle. It was not built for any other purpose than to look beautiful and magnificent, and this it does to perfection!

To Schönbrunn came statesmen, princes, great leaders from all over Europe. But perhaps the most important visitor was a little boy of seven, and he came to play the piano: to entertain Empress Maria Theresa and her family of sixteen children. His name was Wolfgang Amadeus Mozart, and he had been born in Salzburg, a town within the Empress's dominions. Music surrounded him from his cradle, for his father, Leopold, was a musician in the court orchestra of the Arch-

The Gloriette

bishop of Salzburg. Leopold Mozart taught his daughter Nanerl to play the clavier, a keyboard instrument like the piano, and little Wolfgang would stand watching and listening. One day he clambered onto the music stool and played on his own, absolutely correctly, the piece Nanerl had just been practising. Nanerl and their parents watched in amazement – Wolfgang was just three years old.

From that moment, his father began to teach him everything he knew himself. He was utterly certain that his son was going to be a great musician, and win fame and fortune. When Wolfgang was six and Nanerl was eleven, their father took his two clever children on a tour of the cities and courts of Europe, and so at length they came to the Music Room at Schönbrunn, invited to play for the Empress herself, and for her family.

It was a great occasion – Wolfgang was very grand,

Schonbrunn interior

dressed in fine court clothes of stiff brocade. He was so little he had to be lifted onto the music stool, but he played his very best. The Empress and her family sat and listened. At the end, he jumped off the stool to acknowledge the applause, but his beautiful new court shoes slipped on the gleaming parquet floor, and he fell over beside the piano. The courtiers smiled indulgently, but the Empress's youngest daughter, Maria

Young Mozart (painting)

Antonia, who was six years old, ran over to help him to his feet.

'You are a very kind princess,' he said. 'I shall marry you when I grow up.' But of course he never did. When little Maria Antonia grew up and was married, it was to the King of France. She became the beautiful and glittering Queen Marie Antoinette, who ruled over the Palace of Versailles near Paris.

Wolfgang Mozart did indeed become a great musician, one of the greatest the world has known. He became famous throughout Europe, and the music he composed is as much loved today as it was then. But though in Vienna he found the fame his father had hoped for, fortune always escaped him. He was always worried over money, and he died a poor man.

In the Central Cemetery of Vienna, there is a monument to Mozart, where he is honoured as one of Vienna's, and the world's, greatest composers. Surrounding his monument are the graves of other great musicians who lived and worked in this city. Beethoven is buried here, and not far from him is the grave of Brahms. And Strauss, the Waltz King, the idol of nineteenth century Vienna, is here too.

For Mozart there is no grave, only a monument. He died in such poverty that he was buried in a pauper's grave, without a headstone to mark the place where he

Vienna Central Cemetery

lay. His grave is lost forever: he is buried somewhere in Vienna, but to this day no one knows for certain where.

Mozart died penniless and unhappy in 1791 – and only two years later so did the little Princess he had wanted to marry. For Maria Antonia, now Queen Marie Antoinette died on the guillotine, in Paris, where she had ruled as queen, when France was torn by Revolution.

The Vienna Boys' Choir

Vienna has always been a city of music – Mozart was part of a great tradition. Four hundred and fifty years ago a Hapsburg Emperor, Maximilian I, founded a choir of boys whose duty it was to sing a Mass every Sunday morning in the Chapel in the Hofburg Palace. This was the Vienna Boys' Choir, and today its fame has spread throughout the world. Every Sunday at 9.30, the Choir still obeys the command of its founder, and a Mass is sung in the Hofburg Chapel. The Mass is usually by one of the great Viennese composers like Schubert, who began his musical career as a member of the Choir.

The boys live and go to school in a Palace! The Austrian government is so proud of the choir that they have lent them the Augarten – a beautiful baroque palace set in its own grounds. Sweeping marble staircases and glittering chandeliers are as much part of the lives of the Vienna Boys' Choir as a plate glass and concrete are for the average British schoolboy.

I went to the Augarten to meet Klaus, who has been

in the Choir for five years. He speaks very good English which he began to learn at school, and has been able to practise during the Choir's frequent visits to Britain and America. Klaus was dressed in the sailor uniform the boys wear for concerts, for Chapel on Sundays, and for other special occasions. They are not given the uniform as a matter of course. It is presented to them at a ceremony by the Headmaster after they have been a year at the school.

Standing beneath a portrait of the founder, Dr Tautschnig, the headmaster tells the new boys that they are now Sängerknaben (Vienna Choir Boys) and that they are not only members of an ancient foundation, but, when they go abroad, they will be ambassadors of their country as well.

Although he is only fourteen, Klaus has been round the world several times. He has been to almost every country in Europe as well as to places like Australia, Japan and India.

A group of Vienna Choir Boys were stranded in Australia at the beginning of World War 2. They weren't able to leave for the six years of the war and by that time they were grown-up and had begun their careers as young Australians. They stayed on, and to this day they meet together at regular intervals, but they don't hit the top C's any more because the eldest is nearly fifty years old!

Klaus told me that they don't have ordinary lessons whilst they're away on tour, but they make up for it when they come back to Vienna. The classes are very small, only about ten in each so that the boys get a lot of individual attention.

The school day is split up between ordinary lessons

78

in the morning and singing practice in the afternoon, with an hour for games in the middle. Although they may sound like angels in the choir, they're as tough as any other school boys on the football pitch. The only difference I noticed is that the games are played in silence. The shouts of advice, abuse and encouragement you normally hear at a football match are missing. That's because the boys go straight from the pitch into choir practice, and an hour of shouting would ruin their voices for the rest of the day.

I went in the afternoon to watch Pieter and Johann, two of the top soloists, practising their parts in Mozart's Coronation Mass which they were going to sing in the Imperial Chapel on the following Sunday. The School's musical director, Dr Hans Gillesberger, was at the piano. The first thing that struck me was the tremendous volume of the boys' voices. When you are used to the pure piping quality of British choir boys, the full rounded sound of the Vienna Boys' Choir comes as a surprise. The voice is produced from the diaphragm and not from the head, and as a result it sounds more like a woman's voice than a boy's.

Dr Gillesberger was stopping them every few lines with notes and comments:

'*Nicht Ky – Ky – Ky,*' he spluttered pushing his head back with a pained expression.

'*Aber Ky – Ky – Ky,*' expanding his chest and tapping his stomach with an air of grandiloquence.

'*Und –*'

Pieter took a deep breath:

'*Kyrie E-l-e-e-e-e-e- iison,*' his strong voice filled the palace, and the crystal chandelier seemed in danger of shattering.

This time Dr Gillesberger smiled approvingly and over the piano the portrait of Josef Schnitt, the second founder of the school, looked down benignly.

When the Hapsburg Empire collapsed in 1918, the Choir and the Court orchestra were dissolved together with the other Imperial trappings. The Imperial Chapel itself, however, continued, and Josef Schnitt was installed as its chaplain. In 1924, after a gap of six years, he decided to start up the Sängerknaben again. Gradually he built the Choir to the position it holds today, and when he died in 1955 he left behind him what some people consider to be the greatest boys' choir in the world.

On Sunday morning I took my place in the tiny Imperial Chapel set in the middle of the Holburg Palace. Admission is by ticket only, and the place was

Hofburg Palace

packed. Only the clothes of the congregation gave away the fact that we were in the twentieth century. The Chapel, the ceremony of the Mass, and the sound of the voices have not changed in six hundred years.

Maximilian I and Josef Schnitt would have been proud of them.

Franz Josef and Elisabeth

Johann Strauss, who was called the Waltz King, is the most popular Viennese musician. He wrote an incredible amount of music: 500 compositions, including sixteen operettas, and above all, hundreds of waltzes. The most famous of all was his *Blue Danube* – and all Europe danced to its strains.

Under the baton of Johann Strauss, the waltz became the dance of gay abandon, of longing and delight, of wine, women and song – of Vienna. Yet during the years of the waltz dream, Vienna was the capital of a troubled Empire. The Emperor Franz Josef, the last great Hapsburg, worked incessantly to hold the Empire together, yet he tried not to show his subjects the problems that beset him.

In 1896, Franz Josef set up a great exhibition in a park called the Prater. The crowning glory of the exhibition was a giant wheel, turning above the tree tops and the roofs of Vienna. The Exhibition has long since gone, but like the Eiffel Tower in Paris, the Big Wheel has remained, to become one of the world's tourist attractions. Strangely enough, it was built by an Englishman called Walter B. Bassett. He made a career in giant wheels, putting them up in Chicago, London,

Blackpool and Paris, but this is the only one that remains.

The Big Wheel was a great favourite and everyone enjoyed themselves at the Prater. Meanwhile the waltz was danced everywhere – in the Winter Gardens at Grinzing and at the court balls in Schönbrunn.

But while Vienna waltzed, Franz Josef worked – all the sixty-eight years of his long reign. He was only eighteen when he became Emperor: 'Farewell, my youth,' he sighed. He was handsome, brave, greatly admired, but he was no playboy monarch. Franz Josef believed he was called by God to rule this sprawling Empire, and to keep it intact for the Hapsburgs. Till the end of his life, he struggled to achieve this end. For this he gave up everything – except one thing: he fell in love with his cousin, the beautiful wayward fifteen-year-old Elisabeth of Bavaria.

Elisabeth had always lived in the country – she loved horses and poetry and freedom – but she came to Vienna as the Emperor's bride. 'I am as happy as a god and as much in love as a lieutenant,' he declared rapturously. But in the grim Imperial Palace in the heart of Vienna, Elisabeth felt suffocated. She was trapped in the dark rooms. There was no privacy and no escape. She felt trapped, too, in the rigid court etiquette. For the Empress could not come and go as she pleased, she must stay indoors, wear formal clothes and gloves all day long.

Even at Schönbrunn with its beautiful gardens, she rebelled against the splendour and formality. Her husband and children did not fill her life. She was Empress of Austria, one of the richest, most powerful and most beautiful women in Europe, but she was never really happy. Riding, once her great pleasure, now became an obsession. She rode to escape from the Palace, from her responsibilities, from life. She began to travel abroad, and lived in Vienna less and less.

Franz Josef stayed behind. I sat at the very desk that he used to work at steadily, for ten hours a day. He surrounded himself with family mementoes, and pictures of their children. Their only son, the Crown Prince, was called Rudolf, and he had an older sister, called Gisela, and a younger sister, too. This last child was Elisabeth's favourite, and I was very interested to discover her name was Valerie, because I had never heard of a princess called Valerie before.

But dominating Franz Josef's desk was the portrait of the Empress Elisabeth. Her picture was never far from his side. He always thought of her, and wrote to her constantly.

'My poor darling Sisi,' he wrote. 'How happy I would be just to spend one hour in your company. But

Gardens of Schonbrunn

here I am tied to my desk, literally snowed under with papers—' She replied with messages for her horses: 'A thousand kisses for the horses. What a pity I cannot always take my favourites with me.' The walls of her rooms were lined with pictures of the horses which became more and more of an obsession.

She had another passion – her own beauty. She was particularly proud of her elegant appearance and terrified of losing her slender eighteen-inch waist. She dieted so fiercely she made herself ill. She weighed herself three times a day, and exercised relentlessly wherever she was staying.

In her own wing of the Hofburg palace she had gymnastic equipment installed. Every morning she would go to it to work on the bars and do press-ups on the rings she had put into the door frame. I tried to reach up to them, but they were too high for me – the beautiful Elisabeth must have been very tall. It seemed very strange, to find a gym in the middle of a richly decorated, baroque palace.

It must have made a strange background for her three children, the two daughters and the Crown Prince Rudolf who was the heir to the Hapsburg Empire. Rudolf in particular was made unhappy by the vagaries of his beautiful absent mother, and the demands of his father's sense of duty. He tried to escape too – to Mayerling, a hunting lodge about twenty miles from Vienna. There, one terrible January night, he shot himself – the only son of Franz Josef and Elisabeth and the heir to the Hapsburg monarchy.

Elisabeth, still beautiful in the black she always wore, was more restless than ever. She roamed from one country to another, as if she was afraid to be still.

She went to England, Ireland, Greece, Switzerland ...
Then, one day in Geneva, a half-mad Italian armed
himself with a knife and waited. He struck at the
Empress and she fell.

Back in Schönbrunn, Franz Josef was still sitting at
his desk, writing to her, before he left Vienna to join
the army. He was sixty-eight now, and loved her as
much as ever. 'I am driving to the station at half past
eight,' he wrote. 'I commend you to God, my beloved
angel.'

His adjutant came in. 'It is bad news,' he said. 'The
Empress has been seriously wounded.'

'Telegraph – telephone – get more details!' the Emperor urged.

But another telegram came: 'Her Majesty the
Empress has just passed away.' 'Is nothing to be spared
me on this earth!' he exclaimed. Then, looking at the
portrait of the lovely wife he had lost, he murmured,
'No one will ever know how much I loved her.'

Bent and broken, Franz Josef ruled the Empire for
another eighteen years. More disasters came: Austria
was at the centre of a cruel war and ravaged by the
fighting after 1914.

Franz Josef was determined to do his duty to the end.
At last it came when he was eighty-six years old. He
contracted bronchitis. One night he was too weak to
kneel at the prayer desk beside the bed, so he said his
prayers sitting in a chair. Then he went to bed two
hours earlier than usual. 'But wake me at half past
three,' he ordered his valet, 'I have so much to do.'

He never woke up. He died in the small hours of the
following day. With his death came not only the end of
a reign but the end of the Hapsburg Empire.

The funeral of Franz Josef was on November 21st, 1916, fifty-seven years ago. Two years later, the great Austrian Empire was finished, broken apart in a dozen pieces. The future was black for Vienna, the Imperial City, where still today many elderly people look back regretfully to the days of Franz Josef.

Blue Peter visits an Austrian princess

When Franz Josef ruled over the Austro-Hungarian Empire, the Fürstin Agathe Schönburg was a beautiful young Princess, one of the stars of the glittering Court of the Hapsburgs. Now she is ninety and spends most of her time in bed in a basement room of her crumbling palace in the third district of Vienna. But she has no regrets for the passing of the Empire. 'I am glad I am no longer rich. Now that I realize that there is so much poverty in the world, the responsibility would be too much.' No regrets but like many old people she has a sharp and accurate memory for the past. I went to visit her in her palace and her daughter, the Princess Lily, showed me into her room.

The Fürstin (Fürstin is the German word for Princess) looked magnificent. At ninety she is still regal and very beautiful. She was sitting up in bed wearing a white bedjacket and a string of pearls. Her white gleaming hair was worn high, supported by a jewelled comb. I was received with a beaming smile and waved to a chair beside her bed. Rather nervously I asked her if she had ever met the Emperor Franz Josef.

Fürstin: Many, many times – the first time was when I

86

was about seven or eight years old and he came to
our town for some exhibition and I saw him. My
father brought him down from the train and walked
a little behind him, and I was shocked to see that he
was just half the size of my father. For some reason I
had expected to see an enormous man, and I was
shocked to see such a very little small Emperor.

Valerie: How old were you when you met him
again?

Fürstin: I met him again when I was seventeen when I
came out and I was presented to him at his Court
Ball. I remember quite well I made a big curtsy to
him – and my mother stood near him. Then he
watched me dance my first dance at a Court Ball
with his – what do you call him?

Valerie: Equerry?

Fürstin: Equerry, yes. He was a very old man and very
funny, immense and with big feet and very clumsy.
When I was fifteen he had said to me, 'Don't forget I
will dance your first waltz at your first Court Ball.' I
was so shocked when he came to me that night to
claim the dance. The Emperor sat with my mother
and watched us, and he said. 'She dances just like
Mitzi.' Mitzi was my eldest Aunt, and the Emperor
hadn't seen her dance for thirty years before that –
so I was very proud. The Emperor knew everybody.
He was so frightfully strict at his Balls, you know.
We had always to waltz to the right, because you go
much quicker to the left, and the Emperor thought
that was indecent.

Valerie: Has Vienna changed a lot since you were a
young girl?

Fürstin: Yes, immensely. The life of the young has

changed immensely. For instance we were not allowed to talk to a man we knew in the street. We had to bow and pass.

Valerie: When was the next time you met the Emperor – after your coming out ball?

Fürstin: I met him when we played for him. I remember we played the Schönbrunner Waltzer for him at the Palace of Schönbrunn in his wonderful little theatre.

Valerie: Did you play a musical instrument?

Fürstin: Yes. I played all instruments. I sang – I played the organ and the piano – but first of all I played the violin. My mother was a very good violinist, and my sister and my Aunt Fürstin Beck played too. Only the people who knew the Emperor would play to him the Schönbrunner Waltzer. Of course, we didn't play as well as his Philharmonic people could have played, but he didn't even notice. And then we made wonderful living pictures for him.

Valerie: What is a living picture?

Fürstin: A pose, you know. In costume you pose. For instance I posed one living picture with my sisters. I played a violin, my sister played the piano, my two sisters danced a waltz. That is a living picture.

Valerie: And you did it inside a frame to get the effect of a picture?

Fürstin: Yes – yes.

Valerie: And you had to stay quite still?

Fürstin: Yes. Of course.

Valerie: How long for?

Fürstin: For as long as the Emperor watched.

Valerie: Tell me about the Empress Elisabeth. Did you ever see her?

Fürstin: No, no. I never saw her. My mother always talked about her because she was so beautiful, and she was frightfully kind and charming to my mother who was really quite in love with her. When she died we watched the train that brought her body back from Geneva. We could see it from the castle – you can see right across the country about eighty kilometres. Usually the train passes very quickly – the Austrian Express. But this time it was quite slow – quite slow – and we saw many little lights there, standing there. They were the peasants with torches and candles. We could see this long line of little lights. It was about 10 o'clock in the evening. And then all the bells rang – you know and all the country seemed to say goodbye to the Empress. Whenever the train passed the lights it nearly stopped – then went on again. No noise, quite quite softly. It was very moving.

Valerie: The Emperor was very much in love with Empress Elisabeth, wasn't he?

Fürstin: He was frightfully fond of her, yes. He was frightfully in love – all his life he was in love with her. And she, she couldn't bring herself to stay in Vienna. She was so unhappy. She liked going out – and she liked seeing people. She was always somewhere walking or riding.

Valerie: Did you go to the Emperor's funeral?

Fürstin: Yes. I was with my family. We were outside St Stephan's Cathedral on a wooden stand. It was a very dark, very dark day. The great doors of the cathedral opened and before the coffin was carried out there came a tiny little boy in white with wonderful curls, golden curls. That was the little Archduke Otto. Then came the new Emperor and the new Empress. The government had tried to stop the new Emperor from walking behind the coffin, because they were afraid of an attack or something. But the new Emperor said, 'Not only we will walk behind but our son will walk with us.' That was to show he wasn't afraid – you see. And I remember we went home to the country after the funeral and my father sat with us, and suddenly he put down his head and wept like a child. You see everybody loved the Emperor very much. He was quite an outstanding person.

The White Horses of Vienna

The Spanish Riding School is one of the most ancient and famous institutions in Vienna. The headquarters are in the Winter Riding School of the Hofburg Palace. Nowhere else in the world can you see such beautiful horses, so superbly controlled, in so magnificent a setting. The Riding School was built by Fischer von Erlach in 1729. It looks like a court ballroom which mysteriously smells of horses. There are three massive chandeliers suspended over the fifty metres of peat floor where the horses perform. The floor is completely bare apart from two small posts right in the centre which the horses pass through when they first enter the arena. Before any performance begins the riders raise their Napoleon-like hats to the enormous portrait of Charles VI of Austria the founder of the Riding School. At first

I thought this was part of the performance, something to please the tourists until I saw a young rider at 7 o'clock one morning in the deserted arena, solemnly raise his hat to the picture before he began his exercises.

Life begins very early at the Riding School. When I telephoned Colonel Handler, the Director, to ask what time would be convenient to come and see him, he said 'anytime after half past 6'. When we arrived at 7 AM, the Colonel was immaculately dressed in a bowler hat, black jacket, white stock, beautifully cut breeches, and gleaming black boots. These were his everyday working clothes. He wears a magnificent scarlet uniform for the performances. Everybody refers to him as Obst which means simply 'the chief'.

I sat with Colonel Handler beneath the portrait of Charles VI whilst the '*Morgens Arbeit*', the daily training, went on in front of us, and I asked how long there had been a riding school in Vienna. The Chief told me that the school began in 1572, so at the time I was there

Spanish Riding School

they were all preparing to celebrate the four hundredth anniversary of its foundation.

The horses originally came from Spain, which is why it is called the Spanish Riding School, but in 1580 a stud farm was started at Lipizza, a little village in Yugoslavia, which used to be part of the Empire, and the horses were called Lipizzaners. After the First World War, the horses in the stud farm were shared out among the states which had previously been included in the Empire.

In 1920, the Austrians set up a new stud farm at Piber, in the province of Styria, for their Lipizzaners, and now all the horses come from there. The foals are all born dark, and become white as they grow older, because the white horses only have been used for breeding for centuries. A few don't go white, but are throwbacks, staying bay or black all their lives. The school always uses one of these, to show that the breed was originally horses of all different colours. The school is the proving ground for the breed, so it uses only stallions, and the best of them go back to the stud as sires.

I asked about the style of riding known as 'High School', and if that, too, had come from Spain. But apparently it has nothing to do with Spain, but dates back to the ancient Greeks. Xenophon wrote a book about training horses in the same way that is used in Vienna today. The art was forgotten during the Roman Empire, and re-discovered in the sixteenth century, and then schools were founded all over Europe.

The main principle of the classical school is that it only cultivates the natural walking mechanism of the horse – walk, trot and canter, and the natural footfall. 'You won't see here cantering on three legs, and the waltzing step which is sometimes described as high school, the haute école, in circus,' Colonel Handler told me very firmly.

The young stallions leave the stud farm when they are four years old, and the training takes about three years. An untrained horse always goes straight to a good rider, and in the same way the trainee rider gets an experienced horse.

'The rider gives a horse what he wants,' Colonel Handler insists. 'And the fully-trained horse gives the young rider the feel that can't be explained by a teacher, that only the horse can give.'

In the old days, the riders were commissioned officers from the cavalry or the artillery, but today there is a waiting list of boys who want to join the Spanish Riding School and train from the very beginning. By tradition, the school never has women riders, but Colonel Handler thinks that women can make even better riders than men. 'They are more sensitive, while men are always inclined to use force,' he says.

Princess Anne was very lucky when she was in Austria on a State Visit, a special exception was made for her, and she rode one of the White Horses of Vienna. I asked about the occasion.

'I think she enjoyed it very much,' Colonel Handler recalled. 'She was very efficient, and I was very surprised and pleased when after I had told her what to do, within a few minutes she was able to do the "passage" and the "piaffe".'

At the School, each rider has four or five horses at different stages, and he is responsible for their training under the Chief Rider, and Colonel Handler.

When a boy begins at the Spanish Riding School he must first learn how to groom the horses properly, then there is a daily riding lesson. They begin on the lunge rein so that the rider need not worry about the horse, which is the responsibility of the man who leads it on the rein. The rider is free to concentrate on sitting properly. First he has to learn to keep his balance in all the different gaits, walk, trot and canter without stirrups and without holding the reins.

Suddenly Colonel Handler broke off his conversation with me to call out commands in German to the young rider taking his lunge rein lesson.

'*Helmburger, Helmburger antraben und Arme kreizen!*' he called.

The rider swung his arms from left to right, to improve his balance in the saddle. Colonel Handler nodded approval. My interview was over, but the exacting lesson continued.

After years of patient training, horse and rider at last reach a perfection of movement which is displayed twice a week in the public performances of the Spanish Riding School. Then the bleakness of the training sessions is exchanged for a glittering magnificence as the crystal chandeliers blaze with lights. An orchestra plays the music of Mozart, of Haydn, of Johann Strauss. The galleries are filled with eager spectators, and the horses enter – just that bit keener than in their training sessions. The riders have changed their brown morning dress for ceremonial uniforms of scarlet coats. The horses move – slowly, elegantly, then more quickly, to the music. Last of all they perform the beautiful movements that make them look like statues coming to life, almost flying: their renowned 'Airs Above the Ground'.

When the White Horses of Vienna show their skill, their beauty and their breeding in the riding school that looks like a ballroom, it all seems part of a court tradition.

The echoes of the Hapsburg Empire are still heard in Vienna!

Piccolo Non-Fiction

Dorothy Smith & Edward Barnes
BLUE PETER SPECIAL
   ASSIGNMENT: London, Amsterdam
   and Edinburgh (illus)   25p
The companion volume to the first Blue Peter
Special Assignment book. This time Val takes
you on an exciting tour of the intricate streets
and fascinating markets of London . . . the old
canals and bridges of Amsterdam . . . and
Edinburgh's Royal Mile under the shadow of
the ancient castle.

Betty James & Denys Parsons
LONDON FOR YOU: A Child's Guide
   (illus)   25p
Whether you live in London or not, this
fascinating and detailed guide will tell you
things you never knew about our capital city.
From the Changing of the Guard to train-
spotting, from the Zoo to Billingsgate, here
are lots of different ideas for days out – you'll
discover that London is the greatest fun!

Jean Stroud
PICCOLO ENCYCLOPEDIA OF
   USEFUL FACTS (illus)   30p
Whether for learning or for fun, you'll find
thousands of useful facts about Space, Pop,
Sport, Nature, Science, History, Money – and
hundreds of other things. It's a real treasure
trove of fascinating information – clear, quick
and easy-to-use.